TAKING ACTION TO END POVERTY

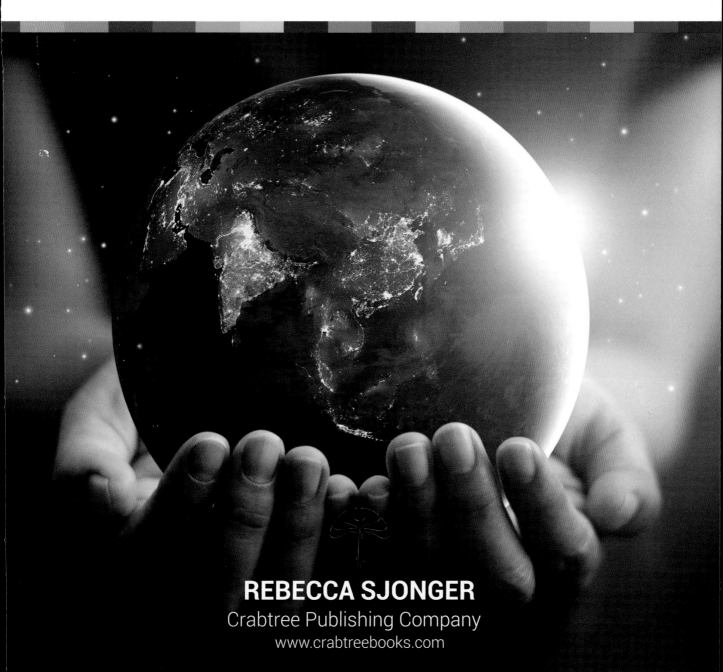

REBECCA SJONGER

Crabtree Publishing Company

www.crabtreebooks.com

UN SUSTAINABLE DEVELOPMENT GOALS

Author: Rebecca Sjonger

Series research and development:
Janine Deschenes,
Reagan Miller

Editorial director:
Kathy Middleton

Editors: Janine Deschenes
Ellen Rodger

Proofreader: Melissa Boyce

Design and photo research:
Katherine Berti

Print and production coordinator:
Katherine Berti

Images:

iStock
RoterPanther p. 25 2nd from bottom;
Devasahayam Chandra Dhas p. 27b;
skynesher p. 28l; Steve Debenport
p. 28 tr

Shutterstock
Valeriya Anufriyeva front cover tr; Drop
of Light p. 6b; clicksabhi p. 8; Michelle
D. Milliman p. 9t; Brina L. Bunt p. 10bl;
clayton harrison p. 10br; anasalhajj p. 11;
Alessandro Pietri p. 12; CatherineLProd p.
17b; spotters p. 18t; Nullaihq p. 20b; Jen
Watson p. 21; Gilles Paire p. 23; Valeriya
Anufriyeva p. 25t; Marco Voltolini p. 26

All other images from Shutterstock

All dollar amounts in this book are in U.S. funds, unless otherwise indicated.

Library and Archives Canada Cataloguing in Publication

Title: Taking action to end poverty / Rebecca Sjonger.
Names: Sjonger, Rebecca, author.
Description: Series statement: UN sustainable development goals | Includes index.
Identifiers: Canadiana (print) 20190134038 | Canadiana (ebook) 20190134135 |
  ISBN 9780778766566 (softcover) |
  ISBN 9780778766599 (hardcover) |
  ISBN 9781427124050 (HTML)
Subjects: LCSH: Poverty—Juvenile literature. | LCSH: Poor—Juvenile literature. |
  LCSH: Social action—Juvenile literature. | LCSH: Human rights—Juvenile literature.
Classification: LCC HN18.3 .S56 2019 | DDC j362.5/7—dc23

Library of Congress Cataloging-in-Publication Data

Names: Sjonger, Rebecca, author.
Title: Taking action to end poverty / Rebecca Sjonger.
Description: New York : Crabtree Publishing Company, 2019. |
  Series: UN sustainable development goals | Includes index.
Identifiers: LCCN 2019023706 (print) | LCCN 2019023707 (ebook) |
  ISBN 9780778766599 (hardcover) |
  ISBN 9780778766636 (paperback) |
  ISBN 9781427124050 (ebook)
Subjects: LCSH: Poverty--Juvenile literature. | Poor--Juvenile literature. |
  Social action--Juvenile literature. | Human rights--Juvenile literature.
Classification: LCC HC79.P6 .S56 2019 (print) | LCC HC79.P6 (ebook) |
  DDC 362.5/561--dc23
LC record available at https://lccn.loc.gov/2019023706
LC ebook record available at https://lccn.loc.gov/2019023707

Crabtree Publishing Company

www.crabtreebooks.com   1-800-387-7650

Printed in the U.S.A./082019/CG20190712

Published in Canada
Crabtree Publishing
616 Welland Ave.
St. Catharines, Ontario
L2M 5V6

Published in the United States
Crabtree Publishing
PMB 59051
350 Fifth Avenue, 59th Floor
New York, New York 10118

Published in the United Kingdom
Crabtree Publishing
Maritime House
Basin Road North, Hove
BN41 1WR

Published in Australia
Crabtree Publishing
Unit 3–5 Currumbin Court
Capalaba
QLD 4157

CONTENTS

POVERTY AND THE SUSTAINABLE DEVELOPMENT GOALS

What would you do without healthy food, a safe home, or even a change of clothes? Children and adults who live in poverty do not have enough money to meet their basic needs. This includes billions of people around the world. Going to school, seeing a doctor, and drinking clean water may all be out of their reach. The odds of doing well in life are stacked against them.

GET TO KNOW THE ISSUE

CRISIS IN THE CENTRAL AFRICAN REPUBLIC

More than 700 million people worldwide live in **extreme poverty**. They are the very poorest of the poor. 12-year-old Jean lives in the Central African Republic. More than 50 percent of the people there face extreme poverty. Jean's mom died giving birth to him. Soon after, his dad passed away from **AIDS**. Jean's grandma is raising him.

When Jean was younger, he helped his grandmother sell goods at the market. He hoped to go to school one day. But the school in his town was destroyed during a **civil war**.

Jean is small for his age because he does not get enough healthy food to eat. There is no clean water to drink. There are no sewers to carry away waste. For these reasons, he and his grandma are often sick. They cannot afford health care. When she became too ill to work, they ran out of money in days.

With no other options, Jean took a job in a diamond mine. He works hard for at least 10 hours a day, but he does not earn enough to live on. Jean worries all the time about what will happen to him and his grandma.

Half of the people living in extreme poverty are under the age of 18.

Many people living in poverty face food insecurity. This means they worry about running out of food, are unable to buy a healthy variety of foods, or must miss meals.

SOCIAL INEQUALITY

When people with less money and power do not have equal opportunities, it is called **social inequality**. This problem has serious effects on people living in poverty. Imagine you and a friend are the smartest students in your grade. Your family often eats less healthy foods because they are cheaper. You get sick more often than other kids and miss school. Sometimes you cannot focus in class. Your parents juggle multiple jobs just to get by. They depend on you to help out a lot at home.

In contrast, your friend's family is much wealthier than your family. All of your friend's basic needs are met—and more. She can put more effort into getting ahead in school. Her parents even pay for extra tutoring. You may be just as smart as your friend, but you do not have the same advantages. The social inequality between you means she may have more opportunities to get better grades, or later, to attend a better-rated college and get a higher-paying job.

A MASSIVE CHALLENGE

The United Nations (UN) describes ending poverty as its biggest challenge. Members from 193 countries form this organization. They work together on global issues such as promoting peace, improving human rights, and protecting the environment. Sustainable development is at the heart of their efforts. This means that what they do must meet today's needs without harming the ability to meet needs of the future.

2030 AGENDA
FOR SUSTAINABLE DEVELOPMENT

In September 2015, more than 150 international leaders met in New York City. They approved an action plan to help people around the world thrive. It also looks after the planet for future generations. They called it the 2030 Agenda for Sustainable Development. By that year, it aims to:

- **End poverty**

- **Increase** economic growth

- **Reduce inequality across all aspects of life**

- **Improve people's lives through better jobs, health care, and education**

- **Reduce** climate change **and protect** vulnerable people from its impact

The UN headquarters is in New York City.

COLLABORATIVE GOALS

Seventeen Sustainable Development Goals (SDGs) are at the heart of the agenda. The UN launched them on January 1, 2016. All of these goals fit together and depend on one another. The SDGs must be met in a sustainable way. That means they balance economic growth, the environment, and social issues. Reaching these goals will shape a fair world in which no one is left behind. This book focuses on how Goals 1, 2, 3, 6, and 8 work together to end poverty. Flip to page 14 to learn more about these goals.

? If we take action now, how many children does the UN think could be saved from living in extreme poverty by 2030?

Answer: 167 million

Anyone can collaborate, or work together, in this global movement.

WORKING TOGETHER

The UN cannot achieve these goals on its own. People around the world must take action, too. Getting young people involved is important. You will be affected the most by what happens in the future. When you are an adult in 2030, what kind of world do you want to live in? You can play a role in shaping that world now!

SPOTLIGHT
ON POVERTY

Throughout world history, the majority of people were very poor. With the exception of rulers and wealthy traders, the standard of living was low for all. The standard of living is measured by the quality of things such as shelter, clothing, and food.

The development of **industries** changed how people have lived over the past 200 years. At first, Europe, North America, and Australia gained the most. People in these areas looked in new countries for ways to gain wealth. They took advantage of the **resources** and people in other regions. Many fought this inequality. The world began to view poverty as something that could—and should—be ended. Living standards improved in many areas by the mid 1900s. Fewer people lived in poverty. However, the decrease is slowing down.

EFFECTS OF POVERTY

Poverty is felt in every aspect of life. Not being able to afford enough food leads to missing meals, hunger, and poor **nutrition**. In some places, it can take hours to find clean drinking water—if it is available at all. Dirty water and a lack of waste removal lead to outbreaks of illnesses. There can also be less access to health care. Getting an education is difficult, too. Time and money are spent trying to survive, instead of getting ahead. People who face these challenges find themselves trapped in a cycle. Without good health and an education, it is hard to get a job. Without a job, it is impossible to escape poverty.

Countries in Africa and Asia, such as India (right) and Chad, have high numbers of people who experience hunger. Children are the most vulnerable to hunger because they need food to grow. Without enough food, they can easily become sick or have difficulty developing and growing.

About 60 percent of people in Haiti live on less than $2.41 per day.

REGIONAL DIFFERENCES

Poverty is found everywhere. It looks different from place to place, though. The **poverty line** is higher in wealthier countries because their populations earn more money. The cost of homes, food, and clothing are also higher. For example, families with two adults and two children that make less than $25,465 a year fall below the American poverty line. But Haiti is the poorest country in the **western hemisphere**, so a Haitian family with this income would be well above the poverty line.

COUNTRIES BY MEDIAN INCOME

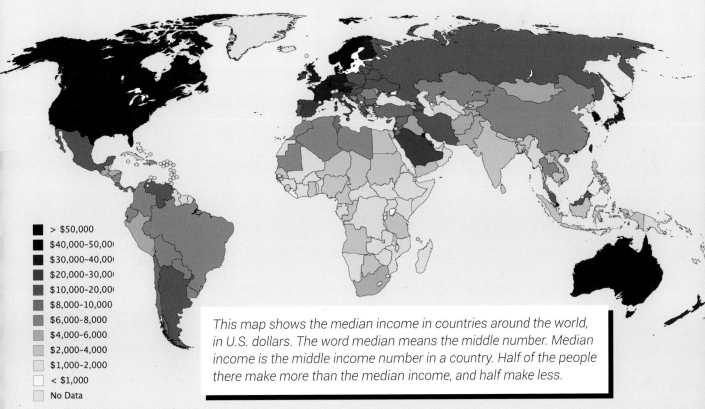

- > $50,000
- $40,000–50,000
- $30,000–40,000
- $20,000–30,000
- $10,000–20,000
- $8,000–10,000
- $6,000–8,000
- $4,000–6,000
- $2,000–4,000
- $1,000–2,000
- < $1,000
- No Data

This map shows the median income in countries around the world, in U.S. dollars. The word median means the middle number. Median income is the middle income number in a country. Half of the people there make more than the median income, and half make less.

EXTREME POVERTY

Someone who lives in extreme poverty has less than $1.90 to spend each day. This is the international poverty line set by the **World Bank** in 2015. Extreme poverty affects about 1 in 10 people on Earth. They are not spread out evenly, however. More than 40 percent of **sub-Saharan** Africans struggle with extreme poverty. Some of the poorest countries, such as Liberia, Burundi, and Malawi, are found in this region. Children there are less likely to live past age five. Lack of **nourishment** can keep their bodies and brains from growing properly. Millions of these youth must work instead of going to school. A lack of education limits their futures.

NORTH AMERICAN INEQUALITY

The impacts of poverty are felt in North America, too. In Canada, 9.5 percent of people live below the Canadian poverty line. More than 1 in 10 Americans lived below the U.S.'s poverty line in 2017. The state of Mississippi has the highest poverty levels in the country. One-third of the children there live in poverty. The social inequality is clear and visible along racial lines. Poverty affects almost 50 percent of black children, but only about 15 percent of white children. Children living in poverty move more often than other children. This is because their parents cannot afford housing. They are also less likely to have good health care or enough food.

Living in poverty leads to high levels of stress for families.

Flooding is common in some states, such as Louisiana. People who live in poverty there may be unable to pay for flood damage repairs to their homes.

*Since conflict in Yemen began in 2014, poverty has worsened. Three-quarters of Yemen's 29 million people need **humanitarian** assistance to live.*

A SIDE EFFECT OF WAR

The many worries related to poverty are also found in war zones around the world. War robs people of safety and security, making poverty worse. After several years of war in Yemen, the UN described the situation as the worst human welfare crisis in 2018. Millions of people there do not have enough food.

Food prices are very high. About half of children under the age of five do not get enough nutrients. The lack of clean water and **sanitation** have led to an outbreak of **cholera**. Young people are forced into fighting, child labor, or early marriage to help their families.

These boys attend school in a half-destroyed building in the city of Taiz, Yemen. Many children, mostly girls, do not attend school at all.

WHEN DISASTER STRIKES

Like war, natural disasters can plunge people into poverty without warning. The World Bank believes 26 million people are affected by events such as floods, hurricanes, and earthquakes each year. Poor people are more likely to live in areas of greater risk. They are also the least able to replace what was lost. As homes, roads, and stores are destroyed, each disaster raises an area's poverty level. Harm to health and well-being are some of the greatest impacts. For example, Hurricane Maria hit Puerto Rico in 2017 and caused billions of dollars in damage. Many people were left searching for food, clean water, and shelter. Youth reported double the normal rate of feelings of **depression**.

Tourist resorts, shopping centers, and businesses were destroyed by the hurricane. Thousands of people lost their jobs and struggled to recover after the disaster.

HUMAN IMPACTS

Poverty can make people lose hope. The poor are more likely to die from illnesses that have cures. They do not have the money and resources to prevent or treat them. Thousands of children die every day from poverty-related causes. If their parents become ill, they may not be able to find or keep a job. Sometimes, having a disease such as HIV or AIDS leads to being outcast. Being excluded is connected to poverty. People with disabilities, mothers with babies, and older people may not get the support they need. The UN believes that the well-being of each person on the planet is linked, so this is an issue that affects us all.

Being unable to enter a building is one way people with physical disabilities are excluded from society.

ENDING POVERTY

Ending poverty plays a huge part in building a world in which people are equal. Creating this equality is a core mission of the Sustainable Development Goals. All of the goals work together to help people rise above the poverty line. For example, decent work and economic growth (Goal 8) make ending hunger (Goal 2) possible. Good health and well-being (Goal 3), along with clean water and sanitation (Goal 6), help end poverty (Goal 1). Keep reading to find out more about these related goals!

THINK DEEP

Why are poor people more likely to be ill?

How is their illness made worse by their poverty?

How is this unfair?

Getting good health care leads to good health and well-being. When a person is healthy, they can go to school and access job opportunities, helping them rise above the poverty line.

13

GOALS
TO END POVERTY

3 GOOD HEALTH AND WELL-BEING

The Sustainable Development Goals are part of a detailed plan. Each goal has its own sub-goals, called targets. They describe the main causes of the issue. A goal will be met when all its targets are hit.

A PLAN FOR CHANGE

Within each target is one or more indicators. They are ways to track the progress made toward reaching a target. Indicators can be measured. Each part of the outline comes together to meet all 17 connected goals.

The example at right shows goal 3, one target that will help meet it, and indicators that explain how we will know if the target is met. If the numbers in this example drop enough, the target will be hit. This is progress toward meeting the overall goal.

TARGET

End epidemics, or disease outbreaks, such as AIDS, that spread quickly and to many people. Fight the spread of diseases.

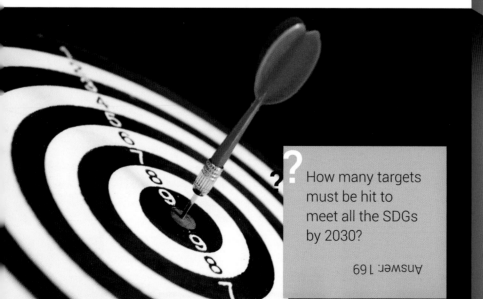

? How many targets must be hit to meet all the SDGs by 2030?

Answer: 169

INDICATORS

A lower number of cases of specific epidemics. A lower number of people who require treatment for disease.

14

This house in Malawi was destroyed by a cyclone. It will be difficult to find money to rebuild the house.

NO POVERTY

The first target of the first SDG is to end extreme poverty. It will be measured by lowering the number of people living below the international poverty line. The UN hopes that number will be less than 3 percent worldwide. Another target is to cut the number of people living in any level of poverty by half. Counting how many people live below their national poverty line is one indicator of success. More than half of the world's population have no support if something goes wrong. They need programs and **policies** in place to help them. Hitting this target is measured by increasing the number of people who are protected.

CHALLENGES TO OVERCOME

Goal 1 faces many challenges. One of the biggest is helping people affected by disasters bounce back quickly. It is hard to reduce the risk of unpredictable events, such as natural disasters. For example, there was no way to stop Cyclone Idai in 2019. About 3 million people in Zimbabwe, Mozambique, and Malawi felt the effects of the storm. It caused about $2 billion in damage. Similarly, when a war breaks out, the region often plunges into poverty. Recovery efforts can be slow and complicated. As people live without basic needs, other conflicts can arise. They may begin to use violence to meet their needs.

GLOBAL EFFORTS NEEDED

The world can help meet this SDG! For example:

- **If the wealthiest nations each donated just under 1 percent of their combined incomes ($175 billion) each year, we could end extreme poverty**

- **Improving access to health care, education, clean water, and other items linked to well-being helps lift people out of poverty**

- **We can spread the word about social inequality and the unfairness of some people living in poverty while others have plenty**

Having access to enough healthy foods is called food security.

ZERO HUNGER

This goal looks at the quality as well as the quantity of food. One target is that healthy foods are available for everyone everywhere. It is measured in part by levels of nourishment. People who are undernourished do not get enough nutrients to be in good health. Goal 2 aims to end all **malnutrition**. This target is measured by an increase in the growth rates of children around the world. Part of the solution is sustainable agriculture. This is farming that meets today's needs, as well as protecting resources for the future. The UN aims to double levels of sustainable agriculture.

CHALLENGES TO OVERCOME

About one in nine people go hungry each day. The progress that had been made to end hunger is now reversing, mainly in Africa and South America. The problem becomes greater as the world's population increases. Climate change hinders the ability to grow crops. Wars destroy farms and make it difficult to find food. One of the most shocking challenges is waste. More than one-third of all food is thrown away! People in wealthy countries buy more food than they need. In other countries, waste is the result of harvesting issues.

GLOBAL EFFORTS NEEDED

Big changes are needed, including:

- **Investing in social protection, which ensures that everyone is well nourished**

- **Addressing climate change, which improves food security**

- **Getting electricity to the 1.4 billion people who do not have it so they can refrigerate and prepare foods**

Insects are a food source gaining in popularity as a sustainable and environmentally friendly option.

YOUTH FOR
CHANGE

Ankit Kawatra noticed that weddings and other big events in India often wasted food. The 22-year-old decided to collect the leftovers and give them to hungry people. Kawatra started with five friends who helped him gather and deliver the food. The youth-based team now has Hunger Heroes working across the country! They work together to end food waste and hunger.

ORGANIZATION	Feeding India
ESTABLISHED	2014
ORIGIN	India
FOCUS	Using leftover food to fight hunger in India
INVOLVEMENT	Thousands of Hunger Heroes

Feeding India now operates an app that lets people and restaurants donate unused food to local people in need, such as these Indian students.

3 GOOD HEALTH AND WELL-BEING

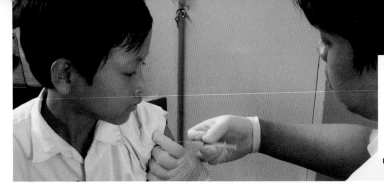

Vaccines are an essential way to lower the number of people affected by diseases.

GOOD HEALTH AND WELL-BEING

Health and well-being improve as poverty levels decrease. Better access to enough good foods, clean water, and medicines have a huge impact. Goal 3 is seeing progress worldwide. One sign is that more children are living to their fifth birthdays. One of the targets of this goal is to end all preventable deaths of children under five years old. It is measured by the number of children who live to that age. Another target is to provide health care to all. It is tracked by how many people have health coverage, and by the amount families spend on their health.

CHALLENGES TO OVERCOME

Diseases and outbreaks of illnesses affect millions worldwide. AIDS is the leading cause of death for Africans aged 10 to 19, and the second-highest cause for that age group worldwide. People suffering from it are often judged instead of helped. This kind of social inequality also affects women. Only half of the women living in developing countries have access to health care. Air pollution is also a global health challenge. Poor air quality leads to the deaths of about 7 million people each year. People living in poverty are more affected because they have nowhere to escape from it. Lowering deaths and illnesses caused by pollution and chemical **contamination** is another target for this goal.

GLOBAL EFFORTS NEEDED

How could the world improve health and well-being?

- **Provide health coverage for everyone, especially vulnerable people**

- **Make** vaccines **and medicines more affordable and available everywhere**

- **Protecting people from preventable diseases could save 1 million children's lives each year**

From airplane emissions to power plants and even charcoal grills (below), air pollution comes from many sources.

6 CLEAN WATER AND SANITATION

Water may look clean, but can contain unseen harmful materials.

CLEAN WATER AND SANITATION

People living in poverty are the ones most likely to lack clean water and sanitation. Almost 2 billion people around the world do not have clean drinking water. Their water contains waste materials that make people sick. This is one of the main causes of death for children under the age of five. Safe drinking water for everyone is a key target of this SDG. They need to be able to afford it, too. This is measured by the number of people who have clean water systems. Good sanitation also prevents diseases. Removing trash and sewage keeps diseases from spreading. Access to soap and water for handwashing is one indicator of this target.

CHALLENGES TO OVERCOME

Earth has enough fresh, clean water for everyone. However, it is limited in some regions. This shortage can be caused by low rainfall. It can also be the result of poor public water systems. More than 2 billion people do not have access to toilets. Human-made wastewater goes directly into local waterways 80 percent of the time. When people drink or cook with this water, it can make them ill or even kill them.

GLOBAL EFFORTS NEEDED

Everyone deserves clean water and sanitation! We can do it by:

- **Developing innovative ways to clean water and stop the spread of diseases**

- **Sharing technologies for public works such as sewage systems**

- **Fighting against the social inequality of women and girls being the main water collectors for their families**

Public water systems treat water to make it clean (below), then use pipes to bring water into homes.

8 DECENT WORK AND ECONOMIC GROWTH

Social inequality can mean that a qualified person is not considered for a job due to their background.

DECENT WORK AND ECONOMIC GROWTH

Having a job does not always mean escaping poverty. Many people work hard and still cannot afford their basic needs. This can be the result of social inequality. Goal 8 seeks to increase the number of young people who receive an education or training. This will help them get better jobs. Success is measured by the number of people aged 15 to 24 who are making progress toward this target. Once people have jobs, another target protects their rights and creates safe workplaces. This is counted through fewer injuries and deaths on the job. Each country must enforce rules that keep workers safe from harm.

CHALLENGES TO OVERCOME

Many people work long hours and still live in poverty. This is a big problem for girls and women around the world. They have fewer opportunities than boys and men. Females also earn less money. Even more vulnerable are people who are forced into labor and slavery, including children. The target to end child slavery is measured by the number of workers who are under 17 years old.

GLOBAL EFFORTS NEEDED

We can achieve this SDG if:

- **Governments and businesses work together to create jobs for people affected unfairly by social inequality**

- **Education and training that lead to good jobs are provided to young people**

- **We aim for a greater mix of people in all workplaces**

Equal opportunity to education is an important way to achieve Goal 8.

YOUTH FOR
CHANGE

Growing up in rural Kenya, Rita Kimani and Peris Bosire saw that it was difficult for farmers to get loans. Banks did not want to risk backing these small businesses. Kimani and Bosire studied computer science at the University of Nairobi. They used this training to collect **data** about farms that they provide to banks. The data can help the farmers get loans. FarmDrive believes more than 200,000 loans could be made to small farmers over 10 years. This is a huge boost to economic growth!

ORGANIZATION	FarmDrive
ESTABLISHED	2014
ORIGIN	Nairobi, Kenya
FOCUS	Improving access to financial help for family farms

Farming is an important business in rural Africa. It is often the only way to make money.

INTERCONNECTED SDGs

Each one of the Sustainable Development Goals fits together. Meeting the targets for one helps us hit the others. For example, jobs provided by Goal 8 help meet the first three goals: No Poverty, Zero Hunger, and Good Health and Well-Being. Plus, when people have enough nutritious food to eat and are healthy, they do better work and help the economy. This is why every goal needs to be met to achieve a sustainable world. This global effort depends on people like you to take action!

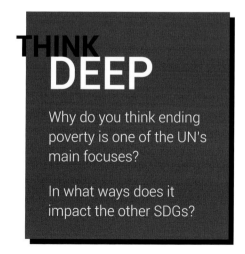

THINK
DEEP

Why do you think ending poverty is one of the UN's main focuses?

In what ways does it impact the other SDGs?

21

COLLABORATING FOR CHANGE

The global leaders who created the Sustainable Development Goals got the ball rolling. People and groups from around the world must collaborate to put their plans into action. We can do amazing things when we work together!

Each of us has our own interests, skills, and knowledge to share. We can pool our time, tools, money, and other resources. This will help us get much more done than we could on our own.

A WORLDWIDE TEAM

The member nations of the UN are working together on the SDGs. This includes countries that are poor and wealthy. They have made commitments to one another and the planet. Each one has its own plans to meet the goals. They need widespread participation, including from all levels of government. Businesses, **civil society organizations** (CSOs), schools, and people like you are getting involved.

Global collaboration is needed to complete the goals. For example, scientists, governments, and farmers in many countries need to work together to develop sustainable agriculture.

This village has received a new water pump. It will allow people to access clean, fresh water locally.

GLOBAL PARTNERSHIPS

CSOs bring together people with a shared interest in helping the public. They do not make a profit and are not run by governments. Charity: Water is a CSO based in the United States. It partners with other groups in developing countries. They work with local governments and businesses to install and maintain water systems. This provides clean water to communities that need it. As it works toward Goal 6: Clean Water and Sanitation, it provides work and economic growth (Goal 8) and improves health and well-being (Goal 3). This CSO also collaborates with global brands such as Google. The tech giant supplies mapping tools and funding. People can also help by volunteering their time and giving money. Some kids ask for donations instead of gifts on their birthdays. The group has received about $9 million from birthday campaigns alone! Young people can also intern at Charity: Water and many other CSOs. They offer their skills in exchange for training. These young change-makers can then start their own businesses that address social issues.

THINK DEEP

Have you ever collaborated with other people to achieve a goal?

In what ways did everyone play a part?

Which people or groups could you work with to end poverty in your community?

THE WORLD WORKING TOGETHER

People around the world are taking action to end poverty. They are collaborating to tackle the connected goals and targets. They are finding ways to help in their communities, in their countries, and around the planet so that no one is left behind. These global citizens can achieve the SDGs by 2030. However, they cannot do it alone!

SOMETHING FOR EVERYONE

There are plenty of ways to get involved. For people who love to read and discuss ideas, the UN started the SDG Book Club. The challenge is to read 17 books in 17 months about the 17 goals. Other campaigns, such as Little by Little's "How to Save the World in 6 Seconds," are for people who are ready to jump in. They post YouTube videos that are meant to inspire action. There are also programs for those who want to better understand poverty and issues such as hunger. For example, A Day in Her Food challenges people to eat only the foods available to those living in poverty in developing areas. The Hunger Project UK came up with this idea to raise awareness and funds.

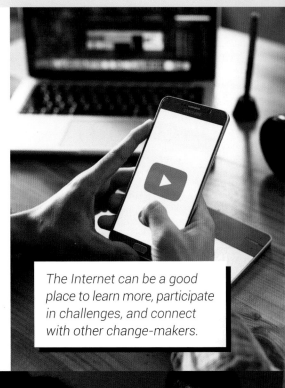

The Internet can be a good place to learn more, participate in challenges, and connect with other change-makers.

Kids can set up their own book clubs to learn more about the SDGs. Try starting with some of the titles on page 30 of this book.

MARK YOUR CALENDAR

The UN and many other organizations attract attention to important issues through global action days. These special events take place on the same day each year. They may include community projects, education, and fund-raising efforts. Here are just a few examples:

APRIL 7
WORLD HEALTH DAY

Focuses on making "health for all a reality" through events put on by the World Health Organization (WHO).

OCTOBER 16
WORLD FOOD DAY

Raises awareness of poverty and world hunger, while celebrating the progress that has been made.

OCTOBER 17
INTERNATIONAL DAY FOR THE ERADICATION OF POVERTY

Annual themes inform people about the many aspects of poverty, such as 2018's "Coming together with those furthest behind to build an inclusive world of universal respect for human rights and dignity."

NOVEMBER 19
WORLD TOILET DAY

Encourages awareness about the harmful effects of billions of people not having proper toilets.

YOUTH FOR CHANGE

Nandini Arakoni was born with a gap in her upper lip, called a cleft lip. She had multiple surgeries to repair it. Later, she learned that people around the world cannot afford to correct cleft lips or palates. Left untreated, their health and well-being are at risk. As a teen, she and her friend Sanjana Gangadharan decided to help kids like her. They began making and selling charm bracelets to raise funds. The girls have helped about 250 people so far!

ORGANIZATION	Side By Side Smiles
ESTABLISHED	2017
ORIGIN	Naperville, Illinois
FOCUS	Helping children around the world who have cleft lips or palates
INVOLVEMENT	Enough donors to raise more than $50,000

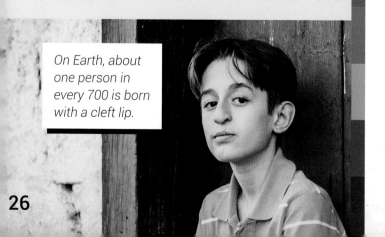

On Earth, about one person in every 700 is born with a cleft lip.

GLOBAL CALL TO ACTION AGAINST POVERTY

Small efforts can lead to worldwide impacts. Graça Machel focused on youth education as a member of Mozambique's government. In 2003, she brought together a group of human rights activists to share their ideas. This led to the creation of the Global Call to Action Against Poverty (GCAP). It now has more than 11,000 CSOs working together in 58 countries. Its major partners include the UN and the European Union. Goal 1: No Poverty is one of its main objectives. It does everything from working with other SDG supporters to planning huge events such as the Global Day of Action and running educational programs. It engages students in ending poverty and getting involved in other SDGs. GCAP sees youth as innovators who can lead the way and spread the word about the goals.

YOUNG CHANGE-MAKERS

Today's youth can change the world! There are plenty of global efforts that need young people's ideas and energy. School projects and volunteer roles can have local and worldwide impacts. Some young change-makers start their own businesses that also help solve social issues. These are called **social enterprises**. They could address one or more Sustainable Development Goals. Check out the Youth for Change sidebars in this book for inspiration.

The word "sawa" means "equal" in Swahili.

YOUTH FOR CHANGE

Sawa World trains vulnerable youth living in the poorest countries to become reporters. They create videos that show the local efforts being made to end poverty. These young leaders communicate and connect with youth in other communities, too. Together they inspire others to create and share their own solutions.

ORGANIZATION	Sawa World
ESTABLISHED	2007
ORIGIN	Vancouver, Canada
FOCUS	Finding local solutions to end extreme poverty
INVOLVEMENT	Over 50,000 people reached with solutions

Youth reporting helps us learn about communities around the world and the challenges faced there. These youth are reporting in their community in Bogotá, Colombia.

THINK DEEP

If you have access to clean water, does it matter if other people do not?

Why or why not?

WHAT WILL YOU DO?

There are almost 2 billion young people on Earth. It is the largest generation of youth ever! These change-makers can work together to solve global problems. You have the potential to change the course of history.

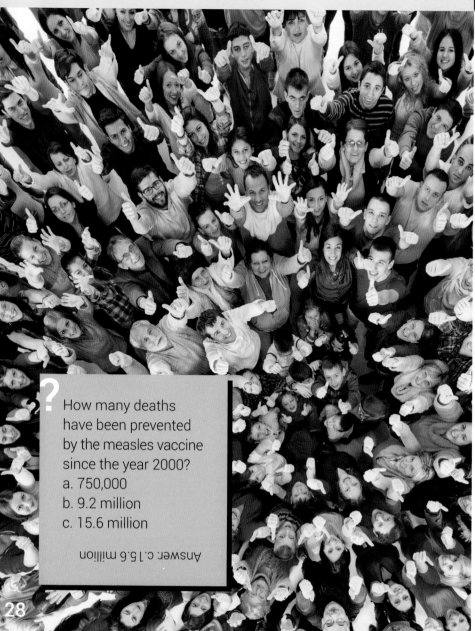

? How many deaths have been prevented by the measles vaccine since the year 2000?
a. 750,000
b. 9.2 million
c. 15.6 million

Answer: c. 15.6 million

REFLECT

Consider these questions to get started.

- What could the world look like in 2030 if the Sustainable Development Goals are achieved? What if they are not?

- Are you inspired by any of the people or groups you read about in this book? Research them to learn more!

- Do you know how poverty affects your own community? Get informed and involved.

- Everyone has something to offer. What are your skills and talents?

TRY IT!

Now that you are familiar with the SDGs, try coming up with your own personal action plan. Ending poverty begins with some simple steps such as those listed below. What is one action you could take today?

- Tell your government leaders that the decisions they make matter to you
- Raise awareness through social media

- Avoid throwing away food—use it up!
- Support local farmers

- Promote a healthy lifestyle for you, your family, and your friends
- Stand up for people when they are bullied or discriminated against

- Take short showers instead of filling a bathtub
- Avoid using the dishwasher rinse cycle

- Buy from sustainable companies
- Find out if your favorite stores treat people who work there well

GOALS FOR THE FUTURE

Global efforts to make sure no one is left behind will not end in 2030. In fact, the SDGs build upon earlier plans called the Millennium Development Goals. These goals were part of the UN Millennium Declaration. It was enacted in 2000. There were eight goals to achieve by 2015. They focused on poverty, education, social equality, health, the environment, and global partnerships. Today's efforts will help shape the next set of goals. If the SDGs succeed, the progress will need to be kept up. If there is still more work to be done, today's youth will be the leaders who decide on the next steps.

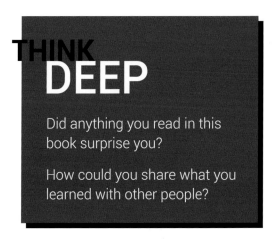

THINK DEEP

Did anything you read in this book surprise you?

How could you share what you learned with other people?

LEARN MORE

WEBSITES

Consider what poverty looks like in North America:
https://bit.ly/1HJ4JZG

Learn about all the Sustainable Development Goals:
www.youneedtoknow.ch

Read the *Young Person's Guide: Changing the World Edition*:
https://bit.ly/2McwYOT

ACTIVITIES

Check out the Take Action on Hunger activities at
http://worldslargestlesson. globalgoals.org/take-action

Play the Go Goals! board game found at **https://go-goals.org**

Try one of the 170 Daily Actions to Transform Our World at
https://bit.ly/2LGK9Un

Start your own SDG Book Club—find details at
https://bit.ly/2EPR9fr

FURTHER READING

Burg, Ann E. *Serafina's Promise*. Scholastic, 2015.

Ellis, Deborah. *No Ordinary Day*. Groundwood, 2014.

Fleischman, Paul. *Seedfolks*. HarperTrophy, 2004.

Mulder, Michelle. *Every Last Drop: Bringing Clean Water Home*. Orca, 2014.

Mulligan, Andy. *Trash*. Ember, 2011.

GLOSSARY

AIDS An life-threatening illness that prevents the body from fighting off infection

basic needs The things necessary to survive, such as water, shelter, and food

cholera A disease caused by drinking contaminated water resulting in severe sickness and vomiting

civil society organizations Community-based or nonprofit organizations and charities that work together to change something to help people

civil war A war between two or more groups within the same country

climate change The shift in global and regional climate, or usual weather. Usually refers to the gradual warming of Earth's temperature.

contamination Something that is impure or polluted

data Facts or information

depression A disorder that has physical and mental effects, such as feeling tired, sad, or hopeless

economic growth Increase in the amount of goods and services produced each year

extreme poverty Severe deprivation or lack of basic human needs, such as food, safe drinking water, shelter, health care, and education

humanitarian Describes something or someone who works for the health and happiness of people

industries Places where goods are created

malnutrition A lack of proper nutrition

nourishment The foods and other substances that promote healthy growth

nutrition The nutrients or substances in food that make them healthy

policies Actions adopted by governments and other organizations to meet goals

poverty line The minimum level of income considered adequate to meet needs in a specific area of the world

resources Supplies or natural materials that can be used to make money

sanitation Services such as clean drinking water and sewage disposal

social enterprises Organizations that use business strategies to improve social and environmental well-being

social inequality Unequal opportunities and rewards for people in different classes or social positions in society. Social inequalities are not natural and are created by society.

sub-Saharan The area of the African continent that is south of the Sahara Desert

vaccines Preparations that provide immunity to certain diseases

vulnerable Susceptible to harm and in need of protection, care, or support

western hemisphere The half of Earth that lies west of the prime meridian

World Bank An international financial institution that provides loans to middle- and low-income countries for projects that are supposed to aid their economic growth

31

INDEX

ABOUT THE AUTHOR

Rebecca Sjonger is the author of more than 50 books for young people. She recommends the many resources created by the United Nations. They are a great starting point to learn more about the Sustainable Development Goals!